MARTIAL ARTS
SPORTS ZONE

# BRAZILIAN
# JIUJITSU
## GROUND-FIGHTING COMBAT

Garrison Wells

Lerner Publications Company • Minneapolis

Lerner Publications Company
A division of Lerner Publishing Group, Inc.
241 First Avenue North
Minneapolis, MN 55401 U.S.A.

Website address: www.lernerbooks.com

Content Consultant: Greg Nelson, Brazilian jiujitsu black belt and trainer

Library of Congress Cataloging-in-Publication Data

Wells, Garrison.
     Brazilian jiujitsu : ground-fighting combat / by Garrison Wells.
          p. cm. — (Martial arts sports zone)
     Includes index.
     ISBN 978-0-7613-8456-4 (lib. bdg. : alk. paper)
     1. Jiu-jitsu—Brazil—Juvenile literature. I. Title.
     GV1114.W45 2012
     796.81520981—dc23                                        2011034228

Manufactured in the United States of America
1 – BC – 12/31/11

Photo credits: Sankei/Getty Images, 5; Diane Collins and Jordan Hollender/Getty Images, 6; Jose Gil/Shutterstock Images, 7, 18; Sankei via Getty Images, 9; Markus Boesch/Getty Images, 10–11; A.F. Archive/Alamy, 13; Masakazu Watanabe/Photolibrary, 15; Jeff Chiu/AP Images, 16; Garrison Wells, 17; Daniel Dempster Photography/Alamy, 19; J. Kopaloff/Getty Images, 21; Frederic Cholin/Alamy, 22; Robert Dupuis/iStockphoto, 24; Kuttig-People/Alamy, 26; Kelly J. Huff/AP Images, 27; Josh Hedges/Zuffa LLC/Getty Images, 28 (top); Donald Miralle/Zuffa LLC/Getty Images, 28 (bottom); Eugene Hoshiko/AP Images, 29
Backgrounds: Aleksandar Velasevic/iStockphoto, Patrick Wong/iStockphoto
Cover: © DIEGO AZUBEL/epa/CORBIS (main); © iStockphoto.com/Aleksandar Velasevic (background).
Main body text set in ITC Serif Gothic Std Bold 11/17.
Typeface provided by Adobe Systems.

# TABLE OF CONTENTS

# CHAPTER ONE

# OVERVIEW OF BRAZILIAN JIUJITSU

In 2011 Brazilian jiujitsu (BJJ) teacher Royce Gracie taught a seminar to students in Colorado. Afterward the students celebrated their promotions to new belts. Meanwhile, Royce picked up the strips of paper that had been wrapped around their new belts. In Brazilian jiujitsu, leaving trash on a mat dishonors the dojo (school). Because of Royce's simple, humble act, the dojo remained pure. That is the way of Brazilian jiujitsu.

Royce is among the top martial artists in the world. He is often smaller than his opponents, yet he still defeats them. This was the case when he won the first-ever Ultimate Fighting Championship (UFC). In the competition, he showed just how powerful Brazilian jiujitsu is. Yet he remains a humble student of his martial art.

## WHAT IS BRAZILIAN JIUJITSU?

Brazilian jiujitsu can be a powerful form of self-defense. The fighting style is very effective. In fact, the U.S. Army adopted the martial art as its main form of hand-to-hand combat. It can also set an example for how people live their daily lives. Royce's humble behavior shows this.

## ROYCE GRACIE

Royce Gracie is one of the sons of Helio Gracie. Helio and his brother Carlos are recognized as cofounders of Brazilian jiujitsu. Royce was one of the top mixed martial arts (MMA) fighters during the 1990s. He fought in the UFC and Pride, a former professional fighting organization in Japan. Royce has decreased his professional fighting. But he remains active in the martial art. In 2010 the online sports publication *Bleacher Report* named Royce "the most important fighter in MMA history."

Royce Gracie *(bottom)* tries to get out from under his opponent during a competition in 2002.

The martial art developed, in part, from jujitsu, which comes from Japan. But the Japanese form, called Nihon jujitsu, has more stand-up self-defense techniques. Brazilian jiujitsu is mostly a ground martial art. This means opponents are often down on the mat when fighting. Brazilian jiujitsu differs from the Japanese style by including a strategy to defeat an attacker. Instead of just learning techniques, students of Brazilian jiujitsu practice patterns of defense. This approach allows much smaller people to defend themselves against much larger attackers. The goal for Brazilian jiujitsu is to use the other person's own force against himself or herself.

Brazilian jiujitsu is a great way to get in shape. Sparring on the mat for a few minutes is a great workout. The martial art is also good for personal development. Success and training improve self-confidence and self-discipline.

Brazilian jiujitsu is very effective when both participants are on the mat.

## WORLD RECOGNITION

Brazilian jiujitsu's effectiveness on the ground has made it popular around the world. Brazilian jiujitsu is a base for people who compete in MMA. Students learn techniques such as takedowns (moves that put the opponent on the mat) and throws. They also learn ways to control and defeat an attacker. All these moves are used in MMA competitions.

A Brazilian jiujitsu school has plenty of action. But there is also peace and harmony. A good Brazilian jiujitsu school can become a second home for students. And the members of the school become family. The school becomes a safe place away from the outside world. For many—including Royce—the martial art is a way of life.

### SPELLING

JIUJITSU IS SPELLED MANY WAYS. THE SPELLING DEPENDS ON THE SCHOOL. IN JAPAN, JUJITSU IS ALSO SPELLED JUJUTSU, WHICH IS THE OLDER SPELLING. BRAZILIAN JIUJITSU CAN ALSO BE CAPITALIZED AND HYPHENATED, AS IN BRAZILIAN JIUJITSU AND JIU-JITSU.

Two students practice their Brazilian jiujitsu moves.

# CHAPTER TWO

# HISTORY AND CULTURE

To understand Brazilian jiujitsu's history, you need to know just one name: Gracie. The Gracie family molded its own style of martial arts from judo and jujitsu. The Gracies got their first taste of these martial arts in 1914. This is when Japanese judo and jujitsu expert Esai Maeda came to Brazil to teach martial arts.

The word *judo* means "gentle way" in Japanese. Judo came from a style of Japanese samurai combat called jujitsu. It was used in close combat and for unarmed self-defense. *Jujitsu* means "gentle art" in Japanese.

## THE GRACIE CHALLENGE

IN BRAZIL CARLOS GRACIE FOUGHT WITH PEOPLE FROM OTHER MARTIAL ARTS STYLES. HIS OPPONENTS INCLUDED FIGHTERS BIGGER THAN HE WAS. AT FIRST THE FIGHTERS THOUGHT THEY WOULD EASILY BEAT CARLOS. BUT EVENTUALLY HE BEAT SO MANY THAT NO ONE ELSE WANTED TO FIGHT HIM. IN THE 1920S, CARLOS CALLED AN OPEN CHALLENGE FOR ANYONE TO FIGHT HIM. THE TOURNAMENT WAS KNOWN AS THE GRACIE CHALLENGE.

Rickson Gracie, another son of Helio, used Brazilian jiujitsu in his MMA competitions.

When Maeda came to Brazil, he met Gastao Gracie. Maeda taught judo to Gastao's son Carlos. Carlos's younger brother Helio could not take part in the practice. At the time, he was too small and frail. But Helio watched and learned a lot. Soon he knew enough to teach. He began teaching in 1925. He brought new techniques to the martial art because of his small size. To develop his style, Helio fought all over the world against other martial artists. He won most of his matches and proved his style was effective.

## THE UNITED STATES

The Gracie family moved to Southern California in the late 1970s. They brought what they came to call Brazilian jiujitsu with them. Teaching the martial art had a humble beginning. Rorion, Helio's oldest son, began teaching from his garage. He offered free lessons to anyone he met.

Eventually, he had hundreds of students. In 1989 the Gracies opened the Gracie Jiu-Jitsu Academy in Torrance, California.

Brazilian jiujitsu got its biggest boost in 1993, when Rorion created the UFC tournament. He wanted to determine which martial art was the best. The first tournament was named UFC 1 and was held in Denver, Colorado. Fighters from different styles and from all over the world came to show their skills. There were no weight classes. The fights continued until one fighter either submitted or was knocked out. Royce was the smallest of the contestants. But he won the tournament. Royce defeated Gerard Gordeau in the final. Gordeau practiced karate and a French striking art called savate.

## POPULARITY

Royce's win was the spark Brazilian jiujitsu needed. Its popularity soared. Brazilian jiujitsu schools are in every state and around the world. Most martial arts schools teach Brazilian jiujitsu. It's a multimillion-dollar industry. Books, websites, and DVDs feature the sport.

Brazilian jiujitsu even has a Hollywood connection. When Rorion first arrived in California, he worked as an extra in the movies. He taught Brazilian jiujitsu on the side. He used his sport to develop fight scenes in the movies *Lethal Weapon 1* and *Lethal Weapon 3*.

**CELEBRITIES WHO TRAIN IN BRAZILIAN JIUJITSU**

- ACTORS ED O'NEILL AND NICOLAS CAGE STUDY BJJ FOR SELF-DEFENSE AND TO KEEP IN SHAPE.

- JOE ROGAN, UFC COMMENTATOR, STUDIES FOR SELF-DEFENSE, TO KEEP IN SHAPE, AND TO HELP IN HIS COMMENTARY.

Rorion produced the documentary *Gracie Jiu-Jitsu in Action* to help promote Brazilian jiujitsu. The film created a buzz about the martial art. In 1999 a documentary called *Choke* was released. It features Rickson Gracie preparing for, fighting in, and winning a tournament in Japan.

John Machado (right) chokes an opponent in the 2008 film *Redbelt*, which is about Brazilian jiujitsu.

John Machado acted in the film *Kickboxer 4: The Aggressor* and in the television show *Walker: Texas Ranger*. He is a highly trained Brazilian jiujitsu athlete. He also produced his own feature movie, *Brazilian Brawl*. The movie included his brothers Carlos, Jean Jacques, Rigan, and Roger. They are all Brazilian jiujitsu experts.

# CHAPTER THREE

# EQUIPMENT AND TECHNIQUES

A person doesn't need a lot of equipment to practice Brazilian jiujitsu. A T-shirt and a pair of shorts work fine. Shoes aren't needed because Brazilian jiujitsu is practiced barefoot. But most traditional Brazilian jiujitsu students wear a uniform called a *gi.* This is a loose-fitting pair of pants and a wraparound top held in place by a belt. The gi is thicker around the neck and front to give further cushioning to a fighter.

The Brazilian gi is slightly different from the gi worn for judo. The Brazilian jiujitsu gi is tighter around the wrists and has tighter pants. This prevents the opponent from grabbing the clothing. But Brazilian jiujitsu is also practiced no-gi. This is where a T-shirt and shorts can be worn.

Mats are also important in Brazilian jiujitsu. They come in different thicknesses. Mats should be at least two inches (5.1 centimeters) thick for safety purposes.

Women around the world train and compete in Brazilian jiujitsu. The woman on top is showing a side control body position.

## POSITIONS AND SUBMISSIONS

Brazilian jiujitsu has just a few basic body positions. A fighter can be on top of an opponent. This is called a full mount. A fighter can be on top from the side. This is called a side control. A fighter can be on the opponent's back. This is called a back mount. Or a fighter can be on the bottom with his or her legs controlling the opponent. This is called a guard.

The full mount is also used in MMA competitions.

From these positions, the important submission techniques are applied. These are the moves the fighter makes that an opponent cannot get out of.

## SUBMISSION TECHNIQUES

Brazilian jiujitsu is all about technique. It is the key to defeating larger opponents. This is why learning correct techniques is very important. One of the key submission techniques is the joint lock. In a joint lock, a fighter makes an opponent submit by twisting a joint. Elbows, shoulders, or wrists are good targets for joint locks.

### ADULT BELTS IN BRAZILIAN JIUJITSU

BRAZILIAN JIUJITSU'S BELT SYSTEM CAME FROM KODOKAN JUDO. THIS IS ANOTHER JAPANESE MARTIAL ART. EACH BELT COLOR IS FOR A LEVEL OF SKILL. THE BELTS IN ORDER ARE WHITE, BLUE, PURPLE, BROWN, BLACK, BLACK RED, AND RED. OFTEN STUDENTS ARE GIVEN STRIPES FOR THEIR BELTS TO SHOW PROGRESS TOWARD THE NEXT BELT. SO A BLUE BELT WITH ONE STRIPE OUTRANKS A BLUE BELT WITH NO STRIPE.

Royce Gracie demonstrates the armbar, a popular submission technique.

By using submission techniques, a Brazilian jiujitsu fighter can defeat an opponent from any of the basic positions. The fighters are patient. Eventually, an opponent will give the fighter an opportunity to apply a submission.

Brazilian jiujitsu students are taught a series of submissions. Which submission to use depends on the opponent's attack. More than 20 submissions can respond to one attack alone. The moves include a takedown, a choke (pressure on the neck) from the side, and a choke from behind. An armbar—in which the opponent's arm is extended beyond its normal reach—is another popular submission technique. For every move an attacker makes, there is a Brazilian jiujitsu technique for self-defense.

The rear naked choke is applied from behind using the arms to form a triangle.

## CHOKES

Fighters use two main chokes. In one type of choke, pressure is applied to the sides of the neck. In the second type of choke, pressure is applied to the front of the neck on the windpipe. The chokes slow the flow of oxygen or blood to the brain. A choke is safe as long as the choke hold is released quickly and blood flows back into the brain. However, a choke is still dangerous. The move should never be practiced without proper training and supervision.

Chokes can be applied from the back, the side, or the front. Diego Sanchez is a brown belt in Brazilian jiujitsu and a professional MMA fighter. He often uses the rear naked choke in his fights. This choke is applied from the back with the arms. A fighter can also apply a choke with the legs. This is called a triangle choke. Usually, the opponent who is being choked will tap out. This is a sign he or she is giving up. At that point, the fighter stops the choke.

The triangle choke is applied with the legs and is used to force the opponent to yield a match.

## FAVORITE BRAZILIAN JIUJITSU MOVE

EVERY MARTIAL ARTIST HAS HIS OR HER FAVORITE POSITIONS, MOVES, AND SUBMISSIONS. ANTONIO RODRIGO NOGUEIRA IS A BRAZILIAN JIUJITSU BLACK BELT AND AN MMA PROFESSIONAL. HIS FAVORITE SUBMISSION IS THE ARMLOCK (A MOVE THAT FORCES THE ELBOW OR THE SHOULDER BEYOND NORMAL RANGE).

# COMPETITION

**B**razilian jiujitsu is mostly used for self-defense. But there is a competitive element too. Competition is a way to show how skilled fighters are in the techniques. Even in training, students "roll" with their partners. This means they practice techniques and defense against one another.

Competition in Brazilian jiujitsu is worldwide. Some famous Brazilian jiujitsu champions include Roger Gracie Gomes (grandson of Carlos Gracie), Fabricio Werdum, Braulio Estima, Alexandre Ribeiro, and Rafael Mendes. Kyra Gracie (great-granddaughter of Carlos) is a top female competitor. She has won several international titles. These include first place in the world championship lightweight category in 2008. Leticia Ribeiro won first in the 2011 World Brazilian Jiu-Jitsu Championships. Top Americans include Hillary Williams, Lisa Ellis-Ward, and Miesha Tate.

In a 2010 MMA match, Fabricio Werdum (middle) defeated his opponent using his Brazilian jiujitsu skills.

## TOURNAMENTS

The United States hosts several tournaments. These include the UFC, in which Brazilian jiujitsu plays a major role, and other MMA competitions. Most local and regional tournaments are not professional, however. Rules and age divisions are set up in amateur competitions. These protect participants by grouping fighters against those with similar skills.

Competitors fight for control and leverage at the 2010 Abu Dhabi Combat Club tournament.

A major amateur tournament is the Rio International Open in Rio de Janeiro, Brazil. The Las Vegas International Open Championship and the Chicago Summer International Open Championship are also popular. The International Brazilian Jiu-Jitsu Federation (IBJJF) puts on these three events.

**ILLEGAL MOVES IN BJJ COMPETITIONS**

- No PUNCHING OR KICKING OF ANY KIND
- No EYE GOUGING
- No BITING
- No HAIR PULLING, EAR PULLING, OR PINCHING
- No NECK CRANKING
- No BODY SLAMMING
- No BENDING SMALL JOINTS SUCH AS FINGERS
- No HEEL HOOKING

One of the world's biggest annual tournaments is the Abu Dhabi Combat Club competition. This takes place in Abu Dhabi on the Arabian Peninsula. This international tournament features grappling, a competition of ground and wrestling techniques. Competitors come from all over the world to compete in this tournament. Members of the Gracie family have won the tournament several times. The latest Gracie to win at Abu Dhabi was Roger Gracie Gomes in 2005.

## BELTS

In addition to age divisions, belt divisions are also used in amateur competitions. White belts compete against white belts, blue belts against blue belts, and so on. Belts are not used in professional competitions, however.

A red belt means that a student has mastered Brazilian jiujitsu.

Teachers award belts to show how they have graded their students. Belts start with white for beginners. Each color represents a different level of ability. Red is the highest belt a person who studies Brazilian jiujitsu can get. Even reaching a black belt can take a long time—up to 10 years. Earning a red belt takes even longer. Most students do not reach either black or red belt levels. It is considered a great honor for those who make it that far.

## SCORING

Judges and referees judge competitions. Judges are often high-ranking Brazilian jiujitsu experts. In a competition, two fighters face off against each other to gain points. Points are given for taking down an opponent and for getting into a dominant position on an opponent. They are also given for getting a knee on an opponent's belly and for escaping.

A fighter can also win by submission. This forces the opponent to tap out. To tap out, a fighter taps the mat with his or her hand. The referee then knows the opponent gives up. A fighter can tap out with feet if the hands are trapped. A fighter can also tap out verbally.

### IBJJF SCORING

THE IBJJF IS THE WORLD'S LARGEST BRAZILIAN JIUJITSU ORGANIZATION. IT SETS RULES FOR TOURNAMENTS AND SCORING. SCORING IS QUITE STANDARD. A MOUNT EQUALS FOUR POINTS. PASSING THE GUARD (CONTROLLING THE OPPONENT WHILE ON ONE'S BACK) EQUALS THREE POINTS. TAKEDOWNS, SWEEPS (TRIPPING AN OPPONENT TO THE MAT), AND A KNEE ON THE BELLY EQUAL TWO POINTS. FIGHTERS CAN ALSO LOSE POINTS FROM PENALTIES. IF THERE IS NO TAP OUT, THE FIGHTER WHO HAS THE MOST POINTS AT THE END OF THE MATCH WINS.

Referees can disqualify a fighter for using illegal techniques. These moves can cause serious injury to the neck or the spine before the opponent can tap out.

## BRAZILIAN JIUJITSU CONTINUES TO GROW

Brazilian jiujitsu is still spreading around the world. With growth comes constant change both in submission techniques and positions. Brazilian jiujitsu keeps its philosophical roots but has the ability to change with the times. In Brazilian jiujitsu, every day is a learning experience—for self-defense and for life.

More and more kids are practicing Brazilian jiujitsu.

During practice, women can spar with men. In competition, each gender has a separate division.

# TOP CHOKES

## TRIANGLE CHOKE

THE TRIANGLE CHOKE PRIMARILY USES THE LEGS TO GET SUBMISSION. TO DO THIS MOVE, A FIGHTER PRESSES ONE LEG AGAINST ONE SIDE OF THE OPPONENT'S NECK. THIS LEG IS IN A TRIANGLE SHAPE. THEN THE FIGHTER HOOKS THE OTHER LEG OVER THE CHOKING LEG, ON THE OTHER SIDE OF THE OPPONENT'S NECK.

## REAR NAKED CHOKE

FOR THIS CHOKE, A FIGHTER STARTS BEHIND THE OPPONENT. THE FIGHTER CIRCLES THE LEGS BEHIND THE OPPONENT'S MIDSECTION. THEN THE FIGHTER MOVES ONE ARM AROUND THE OPPONENT'S NECK AND GRABS THAT ARM WITH THE OTHER ARM. THIS FORMS A TIGHT LOCK AROUND THE OPPONENT'S NECK.

In the 1990s, the U.S. Army began looking at forms of martial arts to decide which was most effective for hand-to-hand combat. In 1994 the army selected Brazilian jiujitsu. Rorion Gracie helped develop a training program, which consisted of 36 techniques that soldiers could learn quickly. The training became the Modern Army Combatives Program. Soldiers learn escapes, chokes, and submissions that are most effective in situations they may experience during combat.

# GLOSSARY

**ARMBAR**

a submission that occurs when a fighter straightens the opponent's arm out, then forces it beyond its normal range at the elbow

**ARMLOCK**

a submission that occurs when a fighter forces an opponent's elbow or shoulder beyond its normal range

**DOJO**

a school for training in martial arts, including Brazilian jiujitsu

**HEEL HOOK**

when a fighter locks on to the foot of an opponent and twists the foot to the side or the back

**KNEE ON THE BELLY**

a position in which the top fighter has a knee on the bottom opponent's stomach, while his or her other leg is used for balance

**PASSING THE GUARD**

the move used to get around an opponent's legs and pin the opponent when a fighter is pinned on the back

**SAMURAI**

ancient Japanese warriors

**SAVATE**

a French form of boxing

**SWEEP**

a move in which a fighter takes the opponent to the ground by taking the legs out from under him or her

# FOR MORE INFORMATION

## FURTHER READING

Gogerly, Liz. *Capoeira: Fusing Dance and Martial Arts.* Minneapolis: Lerner
Publications Company, 2012.

Gracie, Renzo, and Royler Gracie. *Brazilian Jiu-Jitsu: Theory and Technique.*
Montpelier, VT: Invisible Cities Press, 2001.

Gracie, Royce, Charles Gracie, and Kid Peligro. *Brazilian Jiu-Jitsu Self-Defense
Techniques.* Montpelier, VT: Invisible Cities Press, 2002.

Gurgel do Amaral, Fabio Duca. *Brazilian Jiu-Jitsu: Basic Techniques.* Berkeley,
CA: Blue Snake Books, 2007.

## WEBSITES

**The Black Belt Club**
**http://www.scholastic.com/blackbeltclub**
This interactive website lets visitors build a sequence of martial arts techniques
and watch them carried out.

**Gracie Jiu-Jitsu Academy**
**http://www.gracieacademy.com**
The official website of the Gracie Jiu-Jitsu Academy includes history,
information on training programs, and news of Gracie fighters.

**International Brazilian Jiu-Jitsu Federation**
**http://www.ibjjf.org**
This official website of the IBJJF includes information on membership,
tournaments, and ranking systems.

# INDEX

## ABOUT THE AUTHOR

Garrison Wells is a third-degree black belt in Nihon jujitsu, first-degree black belt in judo, third-degree black belt in Goju-ryu karate, and first-degree black belt in kobudo. He is also an award-winning journalist and writer. Wells lives in Colorado.